THE
FUNERAL SERVICES

CW00952102

Reprinted from
Common Order 1994
with an Introduction

CHURCH OF SCOTLAND
PANEL ON WORSHIP

SAINT ANDREW PRESS
EDINBURGH

First published in 1997 by
SAINT ANDREW PRESS
121 George Street, Edinburgh EH2 4YN

on behalf of the
PANEL ON WORSHIP
of the CHURCH OF SCOTLAND

Copyright © *Panel on Worship of the Church of Scotland* 1997

ISBN 0 86153 243 0

All rights reserved. No part of this publication may be reproduced or transmitted in any form or by any means, electronic or mechanical, including photocopy, recording, or information storage and retrieval system, without permission in writing from the publisher. This book is sold, subject to the condition that it shall not, by way of trade or otherwise, be lent, re-sold, hired out or otherwise circulated without the publisher's prior consent.

British Library Cataloguing in Publication Data
A catalogue record for
this book is available
from the British Library

ISBN 0861532430

This book has been set in 10 pt Times Roman.

Book design by Mark Blackadder.
Typesetting by Lesley A Taylor.
Printed and **bound** by Armstrong Printing Ltd., Lornshill, Alloa FK10 2EX

Contents

The Funeral Services

Introduction

This pamphlet contains all the Orders for Funeral Services provided in *Common Order* 1994, together with the comprehensive compilation of suitable Scripture Readings and the considerable number of additional prayers included in that publication.

The two main orders differ somewhat in style and language and may be found useful in different circumstances. For example, the 'First Order' may be found to have a dignity and formality suitable for a more 'public' occasion, while the 'Second Order' may be helpful in more intimate surroundings, when perhaps all present know each other well, or where the family may not be familiar with traditional Christian beliefs and formulations.

The remaining orders are designed to respond to specific pastoral situations – where there has been additional cause for distress, or where the funeral is for a child, or for a child that has been still-born. In these cases, sentences, readings, and prayers attempt to reflect and address the particular grief and bewilderment of such a time. There is also an order for the interment and scattering of ashes.

The shape of these Orders, corresponding to that of a normal morning service, suggests that it is in a full act of worship that the memory of those who have died can best be honoured and the needs of the mourners met.

More consideration should perhaps be given to holding the funeral in the church rather than in the cramped conditions of the home or the more anonymous setting of a crematorium. It is an opportunity for the parish church to offer hospitality to the family, as well as to the wider community, at a time of trauma. In this case, a ceremony at a crematorium would be quite brief, perhaps consisting only of the Committal (see 10-12 in the 'First Order').

In using these Orders, there is scope for the incorporation of other suitable material. For example, some may prefer to add words of confession in the opening prayer, especially in situations where there was no proper leave-taking, where a sense of guilt remains, or where the resolution of differences had not been effected.

In any substitution, care should be taken with language, which should be both evocative and dignified. Dignity can be both a refuge and a relief for those who mourn. Shock may prevent mourners from understanding the full meaning of what is said, but beauty and sincerity of language may help bring peace, stillness, and a receptivity to the God who heals. The minister's tone of voice and general bearing can be of great assistance, conveying sympathy, sensitivity, and hope.

The purpose of the funeral service is not only to assist people to give thanks for a person's life but also to acknowledge God's gift of life, to witness to the faithfulness of God in both life and death, and to point to the eternal life which is ours in Christ. It is therefore appropriate that a brief exposition of the passages read be offered. Some may combine this with a tribute to the deceased person. In this case, care will be taken not only to acknowledge the virtues and achievements of the deceased person but also to recognise the grace of God in a human life.

However, a separate tribute may be offered before the prayers of thanksgiving (see note at the beginning of the

'First Order'). It is important that such a tribute be realistic and recognisable.

Where a prayer of thanksgiving arises from the minister's knowledge of the deceased person, or from information gleaned from members of the family, a separate tribute may not be necessary, although care should be taken not to make the prayer sound like a tribute in disguise. The minister will make sure that the name used to refer to the deceased person is the one familiar to the mourners; it is, however, appropriate that at the point of Committal the formal (baptismal) name of the person should be used.

First Order
for a
Funeral Service

The address at no. 5, which may include reference by way of tribute to the deceased, should proclaim the Gospel of the Resurrection. Any separate tribute may be added before the Prayers at no. 6.

1 CALL TO WORSHIP

The minister says:

The grace of our Lord Jesus Christ,
and the love of God,
and the fellowship of the Holy Spirit
be with you all. ***Amen.***

2 Corinthians 13: 14

*One or more of the following sentences
may be used:*

I shall not fail you or forsake you,
says the Lord.

Joshua 1: 5

Jesus said, I will be with you always,
to the end of time.

St Matthew 28: 20

In the tender compassion of our God
the dawn from heaven will break upon us,
to shine on those who live in darkness,

under the shadow of death,
and to guide our feet into the way of peace.

St Luke 1: 78 - 79

Blessed are the sorrowful;
they shall find consolation.   *St Matthew 5: 4*

The eternal God is our refuge,
and underneath are the everlasting arms.

Deuteronomy 33: 27 (AV)

Praised be the God and Father
of our Lord Jesus Christ!
In his great mercy by the resurrection
of Jesus Christ from the dead,
he gave us a new birth into a living hope.

1 Peter 1: 3

One thing I ask of the Lord,
it is the one thing that I seek;
that I may dwell in the house of the Lord
all the days of my life,
to gaze on the beauty of the Lord
and to seek him in his temple.   *Psalm 27: 4*

Things beyond our seeing,
things beyond our hearing,
things beyond our imagining,
have all been prepared by God
for those who love him.   *1 Corinthians 2: 9*

In his favour there is life.
Tears may linger at nightfall,
but rejoicing comes in the morning.

Psalm 30: 5

We all know that God's judgement is just;
and do you imagine
that you will escape the judgement of God?

Romans 2: 2, 3

Our help is in the name of the Lord,
maker of heaven and earth.

Psalm 124: 8

The souls of the righteous are in God's hands;
no torment will touch them.
They are at peace.

Wisdom 3: 1, 3

Let us worship God.

2 HYMN

3 PRAYERS

The minister says:

Let us pray.

Lord of life and conqueror of death,
you are our help in every time of trouble.
In the presence of death,
you comfort those who mourn.
We bow before you,
believing you bear our grief
and share our sense of loss.
Give us grace to worship you,
and to trust in your goodness and mercy.
Assure us that because Christ lives,
we shall live also;
through the same Jesus Christ our Lord.

Loving God,
in our pain,
we remember with sorrow
how we have failed one another
and grieved your heart.
In your kindness,
forgive our past sins,
set us free from guilt,
and make us strong to live our lives in love;
through Jesus Christ your Son our Saviour.

God of grace and power,
send your Holy Spirit among us,
that we may hear your promises
and know them to be true,
and so receive the comfort and peace they bring;
through Jesus Christ our Lord.

Amen.

4 SCRIPTURE READINGS

The minister says:

Lord, to whom shall we go?
Your words are words of eternal life.

St John 6: 68

Hear the Word of God.

OLD TESTAMENT

A PSALM *sung or read*

NEW TESTAMENT *ending with a Gospel*

5 ADDRESS

6 PRAYERS

The minister says:

Let us pray.

God of all grace,
we thank you that you sent your Son, Jesus,
to break the power of death
and bring life and immortality to light
through the gospel.
He shared our life,
took upon himself our death,
and opened the kingdom of heaven
to all believers.
Look not on us:
but look on us as found in him,
and bring us safely through the judgement
to the joy and peace of your presence.

Eternal God,
you hold all souls in life.
We praise you for those
who have shared this earthly life with us,
and have entered into eternal life with you.
Especially, we thank you for *N* . . . ,
for all that made *him* special,
all that you gave *him* and accomplished in *him*,
all that *he* meant
to those who knew and loved *him*.

We remember with gratitude . . .
(*particular qualities and gifts may be mentioned*)

(*Thanks may also be given for care and kindness
shown to N . . .*)

And now we thank you that for *N* . . .
all pain and suffering are ended,
and that death itself is conquered.
Help us to release *him* into your care and keeping,
in the confidence that all life
finds its fulfilment with you
in the joy of your everlasting kingdom.

We commend to you
those who will miss *N* . . . most
in the days to come
because they loved *him* best,
especially *X* . . . , and *Y* . . . , and *Z* . . . ,
and all the members of *his* family.
Grant that, casting every care on you,
they may know the consolation of your love.

God of all comfort,
in the midst of pain
heal us with your love;
in the darkness of sorrow
shine upon us as the morning star.
Awaken in us the spirit of mercy,
that, as we feel the pain of others,
we may share with them
the comfort we receive from you.
Bring us, at the last, with all your people
into the kingdom of your glory,
where death itself is ended,
and every tear is wiped from every eye.

To you, Father, Son, and Holy Spirit,
be glory both now and for all eternity.

Amen.

Our Father . . .

7   HYMN

8   COMMENDATION

The minister says:

> Let us commend our *brother N* . . .
> to the mercy of God our Maker and Redeemer.

> Let us pray.

> Gracious God,
> by your power you gave us life,
> and in your love you are giving us new life
> in Jesus Christ.
> We entrust *N* . . . to your safe keeping,
> in the faith of Jesus Christ your Son our Lord,
> who died and rose again to save us,
> and to bring us all
> to a joyful resurrection
> and the glory of your eternal kingdom.
>
> **Amen.**

> Rest eternal grant unto *him*, O Lord.
> And let light perpetual shine upon *him*.   **Amen.**

9   *If the Committal is to take place elsewhere, this part
    of the service may end with an Ascription of Glory,
    followed by a Blessing.*

ASCRIPTION OF GLORY

> ***Glory to the Father, to the Son,
> and to the Holy Spirit;
> as it was in the beginning, is now,
> and shall be for ever.***   ***Amen.***

or

The minister may say:

Now to the One who can keep you from falling,
and set you in the presence of his glory,
jubilant and above reproach,
to the only God our Saviour,
be glory and majesty, power and authority,
through Jesus Christ our Lord.

Amen.

BLESSING

The peace of God,
which is beyond all understanding,
guard your hearts and your thoughts
in Christ Jesus.
And the blessing of God,
Father, Son, and Holy Spirit,
be with you, now and for ever more.

Amen.

THE COMMITTAL

10   SCRIPTURE SENTENCES

One or more of the following sentences may be said:

We exult in the hope of the divine glory
which is to be ours.
Such hope is no fantasy:
through the Holy Spirit,
God's love has flooded our hearts.

Romans 5: 2, 5

We brought nothing into this world,
and we can take nothing out.

1 Timothy 6: 7

The Lord gives, and the Lord takes away;
blessed be the name of the Lord.

Job 1: 21

As in Adam all die,
so in Christ all will be brought to life.

1 Corinthians 15: 22

Do not be afraid.
I am the first and the last, says the Lord,
and I am the living One;
I was dead and now I am alive for evermore.

Revelation 1: 8, 17 - 18

You were buried with Christ in baptism,
and in that baptism you were raised with him.
And although you were dead because of your sins,
God has brought you to life with Christ.

Colossians 2: 12, 13

If we died with Christ, we shall live with him;
if we endure, we shall reign with him.
If we are faithless, he remains faithful.

2 Timothy 2: 11, 12, 13

There is nothing in death or life,
in the world as it is, or the world as it shall be,
nothing in all creation that can separate us
from the love of God in Christ Jesus our Lord.

Romans 8: 38, 39

Jesus said,
For the moment you are sad;
but I shall see you again,
and then you will be joyful,
and no one shall rob you of your joy.

St John 16: 22

Jesus said,
Because I live, you too will live.

St John 14: 19

Jesus said,
I am the resurrection and the life.
Whoever has faith in me shall live,
even though he dies;
and no one who lives and has faith in me
shall ever die.

St John 11: 25 - 26

11   COMMITTAL

The minister says:

at the grave
We have entrusted our *brother, N . . . ,*
to God's merciful keeping.
We now commit *his* body to the ground,
earth to earth, ashes to ashes, dust to dust,
in the sure and certain hope
of the resurrection to eternal life,
through our Lord Jesus Christ,
who died, was buried,
and rose again for us,
and is alive and reigns for evermore.

Amen.

in the crematorium
> We have entrusted our *brother, N . . .*,
> to God's merciful keeping.
> We now commit *his* body to be cremated,
> ashes to ashes, dust to dust,
> in the sure and certain hope
> of the resurrection to eternal life,
> through our Lord Jesus Christ,
> who died, was buried,
> and rose again for us,
> and is alive and reigns for evermore.

Amen.

after a brief silence, the minister may say:

> Now, Lord, let your servant go in peace:
> your word has been fulfilled.
> My own eyes have seen the salvation
> which you have prepared
> in the sight of every people:
> a light to reveal you to the nations
> and the glory of your people Israel.

> Let us pray.

> God of grace and peace,
> in your Son, Jesus Christ,
> you have given us new birth into a living hope.
> Strengthen us now to live
> in the power of the resurrection,
> and keep us united with our loved one
> and with all your people in heaven and on earth,
> from whom in death we are not divided.
> For you live and reign for ever and ever.

Amen.

12 BLESSING

The minister says:

The peace of God,
which is beyond all understanding,
guard your hearts and your thoughts
in Christ Jesus.

And the blessing of God,
Father, Son, and Holy Spirit,
be with you, now and for evermore.

Amen.

Second Order
for a
Funeral Service

1 INTRODUCTION

The minister says:

> We meet to give thanks for *N . . .* ,
> who has gone on before us
> into the world of God's eternal light.

> While we are glad for *her,*
> we feel the sadness of the parting;
> and our loving sympathy goes out
> to *X . . .* and *Y . . .* and all the family.

> Death is always a mystery
> [more so when it comes
> unexpectedly and suddenly].
> Whenever it comes,
> it is never the end, but is always a beginning.
> We know this because Jesus went down
> into the darkness of death,
> and came back from it
> like the sun in full strength.

> The death and resurrection of Jesus
> lead to the glory of the morning.
> We follow him through the door of death
> into a life of perfection and peace,
> the life of God himself.

Let us worship God.

2   HYMN

3   PRAYERS

The minister says:

Let us pray.

Living God,
you have lit the day with the sun's light
and the midnight with shining stars.
Lighten our hearts with the bright beams
of the Sun of Righteousness
risen with healing in his wings,
Jesus Christ our Lord.
And so preserve us in the doing of your will,
that at the last we may shine
as the stars for ever;
through the same Jesus Christ our Lord.

Amen.

Heavenly Father,
you have not made us for darkness and death,
but for life with you for ever.
Without you, we have nothing to hope for;
with you, we have nothing to fear.
Speak to us now your words of eternal life.
Lift us from anxiety and guilt
to the light and peace of your presence,
and set the glory of your love before us;
through Jesus Christ our Lord.

Amen.

4   SCRIPTURE READINGS

5   ADDRESS

6   PRAYERS

The minister says:

Let us pray.

Almighty God,
you are the author of life and the giver of victory.
You deliver our eyes from tears,
our feet from falling,
and our souls from death.

In your love for the world
you gave your Son to be our Saviour,
to live our life,
to bear our griefs,
to die our death upon the cross.
You brought him back from death
with power and glory,
and gave him full authority
in heaven and on earth.

We thank you that he conquered
sin and death for us
and opened to us the gate of everlasting life.
We praise you for the great company
of the faithful
whom he has brought through death
to behold your face in glory,
and for those among them
whom we have known and loved,
especially your servant *N* . . .
We praise you
for all the tender and precious memories

she leaves behind.
Now that you have called *her* to yourself,
help us to learn to be content
to release *her* to you,
her Father and our Father.

We trust in your unending mercy
and commend *her* to your care.
Rest eternal grant unto *her*, O Lord.
And let light perpetual shine upon *her*.

God and Father of us all,
by all your dealings with us,
whether of joy or sorrow,
bring us closer to one another and to you.
Help us to walk amid the things of this world
with our eyes wide open to your glory.

Make us sure in every sorrow
that you are still loving us,
sure in every darkness
that you are still guiding us,
sure in death
that you are giving us life for evermore.

To your loving care
we commend those who mourn,
especially *X* . . . and *Y* . . . , and all the family.
Sustain them in the days to come
with treasured memories of the past
and radiant hopes for the future.
And bring us all at the last to fullness of life
with your saints in the kingdom of heaven;
through Jesus Christ our Lord.   ***Amen.***

   Our Father . . .

7   HYMN

8   COMMITTAL

The minister says:

Our Lord Jesus Christ said,

'I am the resurrection and the life.
Whoever has faith in me shall live,
even though he dies;
and no one who lives and has faith in me
shall ever die.'   *St John 11: 25 - 26*

at the grave
We have entrusted our *sister*, *N* . . . ,
into the hands of God.
We therefore commit *her* body to the ground,
earth to earth, ashes to ashes, dust to dust,
in the sure and certain hope
of the resurrection to eternal life,
through our Lord Jesus Christ,
who died, was buried,
and rose again for us,
and is alive and reigns for evermore.

at the crematorium
We have entrusted our *sister*, *N* . . . ,
into the hands of God.
We therefore commit *her* body to be cremated,
ashes to ashes, dust to dust,
in the sure and certain hope
of the resurrection to eternal life,
through our Lord Jesus Christ,
who died, was buried,
and rose again for us,

and is alive and reigns for evermore.

God will show us the path of life;
in his presence is fullness of joy,
at his right hand
there are pleasures for evermore.   *Psalm 16: 11*

Let us pray.

Eternal God,
in Jesus Christ
you have given to us a true faith and a sure hope.
Help us to live
as those who believe and trust in
the communion of saints,
the forgiveness of sins,
and the resurrection to eternal life.
Strengthen this faith and hope in us
all the days of our life;
then bring us at our last awakening
to the house and gate of heaven,
to enter into that gate
and to dwell in that house,
where we shall be one with you
and with all your saints for ever;
through Jesus Christ our Lord.   ***Amen.***

9 BLESSING

The minister says:

Go forth in the peace of God.

And the blessing of God almighty,
Father, Son, and Holy Spirit,
be with you all.   ***Amen.***

Scripture Readings
for
Funeral Services

Every being born of woman
is short-lived and full of trouble.
He blossoms like a flower and withers away;
fleeting as a shadow, he does not endure.
Truly the days of such a one's life
are determined
and the number of his months is known to you;
you have laid down a limit
which cannot be exceeded.

Job 14: 1 - 2, 5

For everything its season,
and for every activity under heaven its time:

a time to be born and a time to die;
a time to plant and a time to uproot;
a time to kill and a time to heal;
a time to break down and a time to build up;
a time to weep and a time to laugh;
a time for mourning and a time for dancing;
a time to scatter stones
and a time to gather them;
a time to embrace
and a time to abstain from embracing;
a time to seek and a time to lose;

a time to keep and a time to discard;
a time to tear and a time to mend;
a time for silence and a time for speech;
a time to love and a time to hate;
a time for war and a time for peace.
God has made everything to suit its time.
I know that whatever God does lasts for ever;
there is no adding to it, no taking away.
And he has done it all in such a way
that everyone must feel awe in his presence.

Ecclesiastes 3: 1 - 8, 11, 14

The Lord God will destroy death for ever.
He will wipe away the tears from every face,
and throughout the world
remove the indignities from his people.
The Lord has spoken.

On that day, the people will say:
'See, this is our God;
we have waited for him and he will deliver us.
This is the Lord for whom we have waited;
let us rejoice and exult in his deliverance.'

Lord, you keep those of firm purpose
untroubled because of their trust in you.
Trust in the Lord for ever,
for he is an eternal rock.

Isaiah 25: 8 - 9; 26: 3 - 4

Do you not know, have you not heard?
The Lord, the eternal God,
creator of earth's farthest bounds,
does not weary or grow faint;

his understanding cannot be fathomed.
He gives vigour to the weary,
new strength to the exhausted.
Young men may grow weary and faint,
even the fittest may stumble and fall;
but those who look to the Lord
will win new strength,
they will soar as on eagles' wings;
they will run and not feel faint,
march on and not grow weary.

Isaiah 40: 28 - 31

Peace has gone from my life
and I have forgotten what prosperity is.
Then I cry out that my strength has gone
and so has my hope in the Lord.

I shall wait patiently
because I take this to heart:
the Lord's love is surely not exhausted,
nor has his compassion failed;
they are new every morning,
so great is his constancy.
'The Lord,' I say, 'is all that I have;
therefore I shall wait for him patiently.'

The Lord is good to those who look to him,
to anyone who seeks him;
it is good to wait in patience
for deliverance by the Lord.

Lamentations 3: 17 - 18, 21 - 26

*The following from the Old Testament Apocrypha
may also be read:*

The souls of the just are in God's hand;
no torment will touch them.
In the eyes of the foolish
they seemed to be dead;
their departure was reckoned as defeat,
and their going from us as disaster.
But they are at peace,
for though in the sight of men
they may suffer punishment,
they have a sure hope of immortality;
and after a little chastisement
they will receive great blessings,
because God has tested them
and found them worthy to be his.

Wisdom 3: 1 - 5

The just person,
even one who dies an untimely death,
will be at rest.
It is not length of life and number of years
which bring the honour due to age;
if people have understanding,
they have grey hairs enough,
and an unblemished life is true ripeness of age.
There was once such a man who pleased God,
and God accepted him and took him
while still living from among sinners.

He was snatched away
before his mind could be perverted
by wickedness
or his soul deceived by falsehood;
in a short time
he came to the perfection of a full span of years.
His soul was pleasing to the Lord,

who removed him early from a wicked world.
People see this but give it no thought;
they do not lay to heart the truth,
that those whom God has chosen
enjoy his grace and mercy,
and that he comes to the help of his holy people.

Wisdom 4: 7 - 11, 13 - 15

PSALMS

The Lord is my shepherd; I shall not want.
He maketh me to lie down in green pastures;
he leadeth me beside the still waters.
He restoreth my soul;
he leadeth me in the paths of righteousness
for his name's sake.
Yea, though I walk through the valley
of the shadow of death,
I will fear no evil;
for thou art with me;
thy rod and staff they comfort me.
Thou preparest a table before me
in the presence of mine enemies;
thou anointest my head with oil;
my cup runneth over.
Surely goodness and mercy shall follow me
all the days of my life;
and I will dwell in the house of the Lord
for ever.

Psalm 23 (AV)

or

The Lord is my shepherd; I lack for nothing.
He makes me lie down in green pastures,
he leads me to water where I may rest;

he revives my spirit;
for his name's sake he guides me
in the right paths.
Even were I to walk through a valley
of deepest darkness
I should fear no harm, for you are with me;
your shepherd's staff and crook
afford me comfort.

You spread a table for me
in the presence of my enemies;
you have richly anointed my head with oil,
and my cup brims over.
Goodness and love unfailing will follow me
all the days of my life,
and I shall dwell in the house of the Lord
throughout the years to come.   *Psalm 23*

The Lord is compassionate and gracious,
long-suffering and ever faithful;
he will not always accuse
or nurse his anger for ever.
He has not treated us as our sins deserve
or repaid us according to our misdeeds.
As the heavens tower high above the earth,
so outstanding is his love
towards those who fear him.
As far as east is from west,
so far from us has he put away our offences.
As a father has compassion on his children,
so the Lord has compassion
on those who fear him.
For he knows how we were made,
he remembers that we are but dust.

The days of a mortal are as grass;
he blossoms like a wild flower in the meadow:
a wind passes over him, and he is gone,
and his place knows him no more.
But the Lord's love is for ever
on those who fear him,
and his righteousness on their posterity,
on those who hold fast to his covenant,
who keep his commandments in mind.

Psalm 103: 8 - 18

If I lift up my eyes to the hills,
where shall I find help?
My help comes only from the Lord,
maker of heaven and earth.
He will not let your foot stumble;
he who guards you will not sleep.
The guardian of Israel never slumbers,
never sleeps.
The Lord is your guardian,
your protector at your right hand;
the sun will not strike you by day
nor the moon by night.
The Lord will guard you against all harm;
he will guard your life.
The Lord will guard you as you come and go,
now and for evermore.

Psalm 121

Lord, out of the depths have I called to you;
hear my cry, Lord;
let your ears be attentive to my supplication.
If you, Lord, should keep account of sins,
who could hold his ground?

But with you is forgiveness,
so that you may be revered.

I wait for the Lord with longing;
I put my hope in his word.
My soul waits for the Lord
more eagerly than watchmen for the morning.
Like those who watch for the morning,
let Israel look for the Lord.
For in the Lord is love unfailing,
and great is his power to deliver.
He alone will set Israel free from all their sins.

Psalm 130

also

Psalm   8
           16: 8 - 11
           39: 4 - 7, 12
           42: 1 - 8
           43: 3 - 5
           46
           62: 5 - 8
           90: 1 - 6, 10, 12
           116
           118: 14 - 21, 28 - 29
           138
           139: 1 - 14, 17 - 18, 23

New Testament

Epistle

I reckon that the sufferings we now endure
bear no comparison with the glory,
as yet unrevealed,
which is in store for us.
In everything, as we know,

the Spirit co-operates for good
with those who love God
and are called according to his purpose.

If God is on our side, who is against us?
He did not spare his own Son,
but gave him up for us all;
how can he fail to lavish
every other gift upon us?
Who will bring a charge against those
whom God has chosen?
Not God, who acquits!
Who will pronounce judgement?
Not Christ, who died, or rather, rose again;
not Christ, who is at God's right hand
and pleads our cause!
Then what can separate us
from the love of Christ?
Can affliction or hardship?
Can persecution, hunger, nakedness,
danger, or sword?
'We are being done to death for your sake
all day long,' as scripture says –
and yet throughout it all,
overwhelming victory is ours
through him who loved us.
For I am convinced
that there is nothing in death or life,
in the realm of spirits or superhuman powers,
in the world as it is or the world as it shall be,
in the forces of the universe,
in heights or depths –
nothing in all creation
that can separate us from the love of God
in Christ Jesus our Lord.

Romans 8: 18, 28, 31 - 36a, 37 - 39

None of us lives, and equally none of us dies,
for himself alone.
If we live, we live for the Lord;
and if we die, we die for the Lord.
So whether we live or die, we belong to the Lord.
This is why Christ died and lived again,
to establish his lordship
over both dead and living.
You, then, why do you pass judgement
on your fellow-Christian?
And you, why do you look down
on your fellow-Christian?
We shall all stand before God's tribunal;
for we read in scripture,
'As I live, says the Lord,
to me every knee shall bow
and every tongue acknowledge God.'
So, you see,
each of us will be answerable to God.

Romans 14: 7 - 12

If it is for this life only
that Christ has given us hope,
we of all people are most to be pitied.
But the truth is, Christ was raised to life –
the firstfruits of the harvest of the dead.
For since it was a man
who brought death into the world,
a man also brought resurrection of the dead.
As in Adam all die,
so in Christ all will be brought to life;
but each in proper order:
Christ the firstfruits,
and afterwards, at his coming,
those who belong to Christ.

But you may ask, how are the dead raised?
In what kind of body?
What stupid questions!
The seed you sow does not come to life
unless it has first died;
and what you sow is not the body that shall be,
but a bare grain, of wheat perhaps,
or something else;
and God gives it the body of his choice,
each seed its own particular body.

So it is with the resurrection of the dead:
what is sown as a perishable thing
is raised imperishable.
Sown in humiliation, it is raised in glory;
sown in weakness, it is raised in power;
sown a physical body,
it is raised a spiritual body.

What I mean, my friends, is this:
flesh and blood can never possess
the kingdom of God,
the perishable cannot possess the imperishable.
This perishable body must be clothed
with the imperishable,
and what is mortal with immortality.
And when this perishable body
has been clothed with the imperishable,
and our mortality has been clothed
with immortality,
then the saying of scripture will come true:
'Death is swallowed up; victory is won!'
'O Death, where is your victory?
O Death, where is your sting?'
But thanks be to God!
He gives us victory

through our Lord Jesus Christ.

Therefore, my dear friends,
stand firm and immovable,
and work for the Lord always,
work without limit,
since you know that in the Lord
your labour cannot be lost.

1 Corinthians 15: 19 - 23, 35 - 38,
42 - 44, 50, 53 - 55, 57 - 58

Praise be to the God and Father
of our Lord Jesus Christ,
the all-merciful Father,
the God whose consolation never fails us!
He consoles us in all our troubles,
so that we in turn may be able to console others
in any trouble of theirs,
and to share with them
the consolation we ourselves receive from God.

2 Corinthians 1: 3 - 4

We wish you not to remain in ignorance, friends,
about those who sleep in death;
you should not grieve like the rest of mankind,
who have no hope.
We believe that Jesus died and rose again;
so too will God
bring those who died as Christians
to be with Jesus.
Console one another, then, with these words.

1 Thessalonians 4: 13 - 14, 18

I saw a new heaven and a new earth,
for the first heaven and the first earth
had vanished,
and there was no longer any sea.
I saw the Holy City, new Jerusalem,
coming down out of heaven from God,
made ready like a bride
adorned for her husband.
I heard a loud voice
proclaiming from the throne:
'Now God has his dwelling with mankind!
He will dwell among them
and they shall be his people,
and God himself will be with them.
He will wipe every tear from their eyes.
There shall be an end to death,
and to mourning and crying and pain,
for the old order has passed away!'
The throne of God and of the Lamb will be there,
and his servants shall worship him;
they shall see him face to face
and bear his name on their foreheads.
There shall be no more night,
nor will they need the light of lamp or sun,
for the Lord God will give them light;
and they shall reign for ever.

Revelation 21: 1 - 4; 22: 3b - 5

also

Acts	10: 34 - 43
Romans	5: 5 - 11
Romans	6: 3 - 9
Romans	8: 14 - 24a
2 Corinthians	4: 7 - 18
2 Corinthians	4: 14 to 5: 1
2 Corinthians	5: 1, 6 - 10

Ephesians	2: 4 - 9a
1 Thessalonians	4: 13 - 18
1 Thessalonians	5: 9 - 11, 23 - 24
2 Timothy	2: 8 - 13
1 Peter	1: 3 - 9
Revelation	7: 9 - 17

Gospel

Jesus said,
All that the Father gives me will come to me,
and anyone who comes to me
I will never turn away.
I have come down from heaven,
to do not my own will,
but the will of him who sent me.
It is his will that I should not lose
even one of those he has given me,
but should raise them all up on the last day.
For it is my Father's will
that everyone who sees the Son
and has faith in him
should have eternal life;
and I will raise them up on the last day.

St John 6: 37 - 40

Jesus said,
Let not your heart be troubled:
ye believe in God, believe also in me.
In my Father's house are many mansions:
if it were not so, I would have told you.
I go to prepare a place for you.
And if I go and prepare a place for you,
I will come again, and receive you unto myself;
that where I am, there ye may be also.

And whither I go ye know,
and the way ye know.
I am the way, the truth, and the life:
no man cometh unto the Father, but by me.
Peace I leave with you,
my peace I give unto you:
not as the world giveth, give I unto you.
Let not your heart be troubled,
neither let it be afraid.

St John 14: 1 - 4, 6, 27 (AV)

or

Jesus said,
Set your troubled hearts at rest.
Trust in God always; trust also in me.
There are many dwelling-places
in my Father's house;
if it were not so I should have told you;
for I am going to prepare a place for you.
And if I go and prepare a place for you,
I shall come again and take you to myself,
so that where I am you may be also;
and you know the way I am taking.
I am the way, the truth, and the life;
no one comes to the Father except by me.
Peace is my parting gift to you,
my own peace, such as the world cannot give.
Set your troubled hearts at rest,
and banish your fears.   *St John 14: 1 - 4, 6, 27*

also

St Mark	16: 1 - 8a
St Luke	7: 11 - 16
St John	11: 17 - 27
St John	20: 24 - 29

Order for use in Distressing Circumstances

The following may be added to, or substituted for, material at the appropriate places in the First or Second Order.

The Prayer at no. 4 has three parts: the general beginning, the specific thanksgivings and petitions, and the section headed 'in each circumstance'.

1   SCRIPTURE SENTENCES

God is our refuge and our stronghold,
a timely help in trouble;
so we are not afraid.

Psalm 46: 1, 2

The Lord's love is surely not exhausted,
nor has his compassion failed.

Lamentations 3: 22

God cares for you,
so cast all your anxiety on him.   *1 Peter 5: 7*

Gladness and joy will come upon God's people,
while suffering and weariness flee away.

Isaiah 35: 10b

God has said,
'I will never leave you or desert you.'

Hebrews 13: 5b

Jesus said,
'Come to me, all who are weary
and whose load is heavy;
I will give you rest.'   *St Matthew 11: 28*

2   PRAYER

God of all comfort,
in this time of distress and grief,
we have come to tell you our sorrow,
and to rest ourselves
within the circle of your love.

Your hands made us and formed us,
and you despise nothing you have made.
Set free our souls from restlessness,
and raise our downcast spirits
from perplexity and doubt
to the steadfast love
of your unchanging peace;
through Jesus Christ our Lord.

                                        Amen.

3   SCRIPTURE READING

My God, my God, why have you forsaken me?
Why are you so far from saving me,
so far from heeding my groans?
My God, by day I cry to you,
but there is no answer;
in the night I cry with no respite.
In you our fathers put their trust;
they trusted, and you rescued them.
To you they cried and were delivered;
in you they trusted and were not discomfited.

Do not remain far away, Lord;
you are my help, come quickly to my aid.

Psalm 22: 1 - 2, 4 - 5, 19

Jesus says,
In very truth I tell you,
whoever heeds what I say
and puts his trust in him who sent me
has eternal life;
he does not come to judgement,
but has already passed from death to life.

St John 5: 24

4 PRAYERS

We praise you, O God,
we acclaim you as Lord;
all creation worships you,
the Father everlasting.
To you the angels sing in endless praise.
The glorious company of the saints praise you.
Throughout the world
the holy Church acclaims you,
Father, Son, and Holy Spirit,
one God, now and for ever.

You, Christ, are the king of glory.
In the tender compassion of God,
you came, the dawn from on high,
to shine on those who dwell in darkness
and the shadow of death.
You overcame the sting of death
and opened the kingdom of heaven
to all believers.
Chase away the darkness of our night
and restore morning to the world.

Enlighten us with the healing beams of your love
and guide our feet into the way of peace.

Eternal God,
our life is a fleeting shadow that does not endure.
Our years pass quickly,
our days are few and full of trouble.
We do not know what a day may bring forth.
You have promised that you will not fail us
nor forsake us,
and that you will hear when we call to you.

Loving God,
in whom sinners find mercy and saints find joy,
we thank you for *N* . . . ,
and for the qualities that made *him* special to us.
We remember with grateful hearts
all that *he* gave and received during *his* life.
We think especially of *his* . . .
(*appropriate attributes and activities*).

after a wasting illness

We thank you that *N* . . .
no longer has to suffer pain or fear,
grappling with death, fighting for life;
and that for *him*
limitations are ended,
weakness is overcome,
and death itself is conquered.

As *he* passes from our earthly sight,
we thank you for the years
of *his* presence among us.
And while we feel the pain of the parting,
we rejoice in the faith
that *he* has gone to be with you,

for in your presence is the fullness of joy,
at your right hand are pleasures for evermore.

Bless those who had the care of *him*,
especially doctors, nurses, and technicians.
Guide and prosper
all who are engaged in medical research:
may they never lose heart
in their search to discover
the way of health and healing.
Grant that by their vision and courage
we may advance in our understanding
of the world
and be better able to help those in need.

after a suicide

We thank you that *N* . . .
is beyond the reach of darkness and despair,
but not beyond the touch of your care and love.
The ending of *his* earthly life seems senseless.
We cannot fathom the anguish of mind
he went through.

Forgive us for those times and ways
we failed *him*.
Help us to forgive *him*
for any hurt we feel *he* has inflicted on us;
help us to forgive ourselves
for any harm we fear we may have caused *him*.

Give us grace to be content to release *him* to you,
in the assurance and hope
that you will show *him* the path of life
and lead *him* to walk in your presence
in the land of the living.

after violence
We thank you that *N* . . .
has outsoared the shadow of our night,
with its cruelty, violence, and pain.
When the trouble was near,
we could not understand
how you seemed to remain far away.
And yet it is to you we turn;
for in life and death
it is you alone whom we can trust,
and yours alone is the love that holds us fast.
We find it hard to forgive the deed
that has brought us so much grief.
But we know that, if life is soured by bitterness,
an unforgiving spirit brings no peace.
Lord, save us and help us.
Strengthen in us the faith and hope that *N* . . .
is freed from the past with all its hurt,
and rests for ever in the calm security
of your love.

in each circumstance
Gracious God,
sustain and support those
whose love for *N* . . . was dearest,
whose loss is greatest.
May they find beyond their tears
unclouded visions of your love,
and may they see beyond their darkness
the clear shining of your light.
Set their troubled hearts at rest,
banish all their fears,
and hold them in the comfort of your peace;
through Jesus Christ our Lord.   ***Amen.***

Our Father . . .

Additional Prayers for Funeral Services

APPROACH

1   Almighty God,
    in mystery you created all things;
    you made us in your own image;
    you love us with an everlasting love.
    Grant us the assurance
    of your loving presence with us now.
    Bear us gently in your gracious hands,
    and bring us in our sorrow
    the comfort for which our hearts cry out;
    through Jesus Christ our Lord.   *Amen.*

2   Gracious God,
    you made us and you love us.
    Your love is our security and our hope.
    We find our true selves, complete and whole,
    only within your love.
    And because in love you have prepared for us
    a destiny more wonderful than we can imagine,
    we trust you with our loved ones and ourselves;
    in Jesus' name.   *Amen.*

3   Eternal God,
    we come to you
    because the friend we knew and loved has died,
    and our hearts are cold,
    and our minds perplexed.

Whatever we may be thinking and feeling,
we know that you will understand.
For you made us,
and in your Son, Jesus,
you shared our life and experience.
Accept us as we are,
forgive us for our lack of faith,
inspire in us a living hope;
through the same Jesus Christ our Lord.

Amen.

4   Lord of life,
in the beginning
you formed us from the dust of the earth
and breathed life into our frame.
Your goodness and mercy
follow us all our days,
and at our departing
we return to your loving hand.
Assure us of your presence now,
and lead us to life everlasting and full of glory;
through Jesus Christ our Lord.   *Amen.*

BEFORE AND AFTER SCRIPTURE READINGS

before

5   Lord Jesus,
as we bow in the presence of death,
stand within the shadows beside us
to bring the light of your deathless love.

Lord, to whom can we go but to you?
Your words are words of eternal life.

Amen.

6   Father,
your love is stronger than death.
Day by day you bring us towards life at its fullest.
Help us as we hear your promises
to believe them
and to receive the comfort they offer.
Fill us with joy and peace in believing
so that we may have hope
through the power of your Holy Spirit.   ***Amen.***

7   Eternal God our heavenly Father,
you love us with an everlasting love
and are able to turn
the shadow of death into the morning.
In the silence of this hour
speak to us of eternal things,
that through patience and comfort
of the scriptures
we may have hope,
and be lifted above our darkness and distress
into the light and peace of your presence;
through Jesus Christ our Lord.

                           Amen.

8   Gracious God,
help us to listen for your word.
Console us in our trouble,
so that we in turn
may be able to console others
in any trouble of theirs,
and to share with them
the consolation we receive from you:
that together
we may find light in our darkness
and faith in the midst of doubt;
through Jesus Christ our Lord.   ***Amen.***

after

9   Lord,
we take strength from these mighty promises,
the strong words written by those
who experienced your faithfulness,
and share with us their assurance.

But you give us more than words.
You give us Jesus Christ,
who is himself your message,
the guarantor of his gospel,
present in his risen power,
to assure us of his victory over death,
and to share with us his triumph.

We thank you for your readiness
to speak with us,
and for your grace to help us in our time of need;
through Jesus Christ our Lord.   ***Amen.***

THANKSGIVING

10   Gracious God,
we praise you
for all that you have done through Jesus Christ.
By giving him to live and die for us,
you showed us love without limit;
by raising him from the dead,
you brought us life without end.
For the assurance and hope of our faith,
and for those whom you have received
into your eternal joy,
we give you thanks and praise;
through Jesus Christ our Lord.   ***Amen.***

11   Heavenly Father,
        we thank you for all the gifts
        of your providence and grace.

        You have promised that
        out of darkness light shall shine,
        light which is the knowledge of your glory
        in the face of Jesus Christ.
        We thank you that his light
        dawns upon us daily,
        and brings us a grateful heart
        and a will to love and serve you
        to the end of our days.

        We thank you for your gift to us of human love;
        for the first love we know at our birth,
        a mother's love and a father's care;
        for the love that unites husband and wife;
        for the love of parents and children,
        and the family circle.

        Comfort us now with the assurance
        of the life which is beyond this life,
        and of a reunion with those
        we have loved long since
        and who wait for us in your heavenly presence;
        through Jesus Christ our Lord.   ***Amen.***

12   We bless you, Lord,
        that Jesus came into a home like ours,
        and knew the loyalties and tensions
        of family living;
        that he worked as a carpenter,
        and knew the frustrations and fulfilment
        of a daily task;
        that he offered friendship,

and knew how it might be a source
of healing and courage at a time like this;
that he went about doing good,
even at the risk of being misunderstood;
that he brought glory
to ordinary tasks and relationships,
and dignity to every human being.

Above all,
we bless you that Jesus went to the lonely place,
carrying his cross;
that he died for us,
confronting all that threatened to destroy us;
that he came back from death,
making us more than conquerors,
and showing that death
shall not have dominion;
and that he leads us into his kingdom
to share with him the life everlasting.

Because he has been with us,
we shall be with him.
Because he has been like us,
we shall be like him.
Because he is for us,
who can be against us?
Thanks be to God, who gives us the victory,
through our Lord Jesus Christ!   *Amen.*

Those Who Mourn

13   Almighty God,
        Lord of life and vanquisher of death,
        we praise you for the sure hope of eternal life
        you have given us

in the resurrection of our Lord Jesus Christ;
and we pray that all who mourn
the loss of those dear to them
may enter into his victory and know his peace;
for his name's sake.   ***Amen.***

14   God of hope and giver of all comfort,
we commend to your tender care
those who mourn the loss of loved ones.
Give them the peace
which is beyond all understanding,
and assure them that neither death nor life
can separate them from your love
in Jesus Christ our Lord.   ***Amen.***

OFFERING OF LIFE

15   Eternal God,
we offer you the past.
We are grateful for the memories
that will sustain us,
even if they bring us tears.
We thank you for good things shared,
and for times of contentment and affection.
We acknowledge also the unfinished business,
the vain regrets,
the guilt and anger,
bewilderment and hurt,
and thank you that in your love,
you can forgive and heal us.

We offer you the present.
You are at work
in the duties that demand our attention,
in the responsibilities that will not go away,

in the kindly words of friends,
in the sympathy and loyalty of colleagues.
We pray for grace to recognise
that these are channels of your mercy,
and to receive them as your gifts of kindness
and of love.

We offer you the future.
It is changed,
because *N* . . . is no longer with us,
and we feel uncertain and diminished.
Yet you will not fail us.
You still have gifts for us to receive,
work for us to do,
discoveries of your unfailing grace
for us to make.
And at the last you will re-unite us
with those who have gone home before us,
in the new life of your everlasting kingdom.

This offering of all our life
we make in the name of Jesus Christ our Lord,
who died for us and rose again,
and is alive and reigns
with you and the Holy Spirit,
one God, now and ever.   *Amen.*

PETITION

16   Lord,
        we do not know whether our days
        will be many or few.
        Help us to put into each day's living
        something of worth, and kindness,
        integrity, courage, and love.

These are gifts you offer us,
gifts that will last,
for they are the sign
of your Spirit at work among us.
We ask this in Jesus' name.

Amen.

17   Risen, reigning Christ,
in you past, present, and future
are brought together in one great hope.
Renew our faith in you,
so that neither the past may hinder us,
the present overwhelm us,
nor the future frighten us.
You have brought us this far;
continue to lead us
until our hope is fulfilled
and we join all God's people
in never-ending praise;
for your name's sake.

Amen.

18   O Lord,
support us all the day long
of this troublous life,
until the shadows lengthen
and the evening comes,
and the busy world is hushed,
the fever of life is over,
and our work done.
Then Lord, in your mercy,
grant us safe lodging,
a holy rest,
and peace at the last;
through Jesus Christ our Lord.

Amen.

The Communion of Saints

19   Eternal God,
          before your face
          the generations rise and pass away.
          We praise your name for all your servants
          departed this life in your faith and love,
          for those dear to us,
          and especially for your servant *N* . . .

          We thank you for your loving-kindness
          towards *him*,
          for all *he* was throughout *his* earthly life,
          and for all *he* accomplished by your grace.
          We thank you that for *him*
          sorrow and sickness are ended,
          that death itself is past,
          and that *he* lives for ever
          in your love and care.

          Encourage us by the example of your saints,
          that we may run with resolution
          the race which lies ahead of us,
          our eyes fixed on Jesus,
          the pioneer and perfecter of faith;
          till we shall come at last,
          with all whom we have loved,
          to the joy and peace of your eternal presence;
          through Jesus Christ our Lord.   *Amen.*

20   Bring us at last to your nearer presence,
          where we shall rediscover one another
          in the light of your love,
          and be given back to one another
          in a bond that nothing shall sever;
          through Jesus Christ our Lord.   *Amen.*

21   Almighty God,
you have knit together your elect
into one communion and fellowship
in the mystical body of your Son.
Give us grace to follow your blessed saints
in all virtuous and godly living,
that we may come to those joys beyond all praise
which you have prepared
for those who perfectly love you;
through Jesus Christ our Lord.

Amen.

FACING DEATH

22   God of all hope,
give us your continuing grace,
that it may be joy for us when our call comes
to commit our spirits to our heavenly Father,
from whom we came and to whom we go;
through Jesus Christ our Lord.

Amen.

23   Merciful Jesus Christ,
we remember that on the cross
you gave your spirit
into the hands of your Father.
By the memory of your death,
help us to live day by day for you,
so that, at the hour of our departing,
we may commend ourselves trustingly
to the same everlasting arms,
and be received into your heavenly kingdom,
to dwell with you for ever;
for your endless mercies' sake.

Amen.

COMMENDATION

24   Our *brother N . . .*
        has gone forth upon *his* journey,
        in the name of God the Father who created *him,*
        in the name of God the Son who redeemed *him,*
        in the name of God the Spirit
        who sanctified *him;*
        in the company of angels and archangels
        and all the hosts of heaven.

        May *his* dwelling place be in heavenly Jerusalem,
        and all *his* portion be peace.   ***Amen.***

COMMITTAL

25   *at the grave*

            We have entrusted our *brother N . . . ,*
            into the hands of God.
            We now commit *his* body to the ground,
            earth to earth, ashes to ashes, dust to dust;
            having our whole trust and confidence
            in the mercy of our heavenly Father,
            and in the victory of his Son,
            Jesus Christ our Lord,
            who died, was buried, and rose again for us,
            and is alive and reigns for ever and ever.
                                                    Amen.

     at the crematorium

            We have entrusted our *brother N . . . ,*
            into the hands of God.
            We now commit *his* body to be cremated,

ashes to ashes, dust to dust;
having our whole trust and confidence
in the mercy of our heavenly Father,
and in the victory of his Son,
Jesus Christ our Lord,
who died, was buried, and rose again for us,
and is alive and reigns for ever and ever.

Amen.

26   *at the crematorium*

We have entrusted our *brother N . . .* ,
into the hands of God.
We now commit his body to its elements,
ashes to ashes, dust to dust.
We place our confidence in the love of God
who never lets us go;
we claim the victory of Jesus Christ
who conquered death for us;
and we take to heart
the comfort of the Holy Spirit,
who carries us through life to life eternal.

We affirm that none of us
lives in vain,
labours in vain,
gives or receives or loves in vain.
Within the eternal purpose,
each of us is worth more
than we can ever calculate.
For *N . . . 's* life as it touched and enriched ours,
we give God the glory.
May he grant to all his people,
pardon, peace, and life eternal;
in the name of Jesus Christ our Lord.

Amen.

27   *In place of the Committal, when no body has been*
     found, or recovered from the sea,
     some of the following may be used:

> The dust returns to the earth as it began,
> and the spirit returns to God who made it.
>
> *Ecclesiastes 12: 7*

> Their bodies are buried in peace;
> and their name lives for ever.
>
> *Ecclesiasticus 44: 14*

> Jesus said,
> 'I give them eternal life
> and they will never perish.
> No one can snatch them out of the Father's care.'
>
> *St John 10: 28, 29*

> Let us pray.

> Heavenly Father,
> we have lost in death our friend *N* . . .
> We commend *him* to your care and keeping,
> in the sure and certain hope
> of the resurrection to eternal life
> through Jesus Christ your Son our Lord,
> who died, was buried, and rose again for us,
> and is alive and reigns for ever and ever.
>
> ***Amen.***

Order for the
Funeral
of a Child

1 CALL TO WORSHIP

We have come together to worship God,
to thank him for his love,
and to remember the [short] life of *N* . . . ;
to share our grief
and to commend *him* to the eternal care of God.

We meet in the faith that death is not the end,
and may be faced without fear,
bitterness, or guilt.

Let us worship God.

2 SCRIPTURE SENTENCES

As a mother comforts her child,
so shall I myself comfort you.

Isaiah 66: 13

As a father has compassion on his children,
so the Lord has compassion
on those who fear him.

Psalm 103: 13

Is all well with the child?
All is well.

2 Kings 4: 26

Jerusalem will be called the City of Faithfulness:
and the city will be full of boys and girls
playing in the streets.   *Zechariah 8: 3, 5*

The eternal God is our refuge,
and underneath are the everlasting arms.
                              Deuteronomy 33: 27 (AV)

Now we see only puzzling reflections
in a mirror;
but then we shall see face to face.
Our knowledge now is partial;
then it will be whole,
like God's knowledge of us.
                              1 Corinthians 13: 12

Jesus said,
Blessed are the sorrowful;
they shall find consolation.   *St Matthew 5: 4*

3   HYMN

4   PRAYERS

God of unfailing compassion,
in your creative love and tenderness
you gave us *N* . . . ,
so full of hope for the future.
You are the source of all our lives,
the strength of all our days.

You did not make us for darkness and death
but so that we should live in you
and see you face to face.
Help us to comfort one another
with the consolation

we ourselves receive from you;
through Jesus Christ our Lord.   ***Amen.***

Lord Jesus Christ,
you became a little child for our sake,
sharing our human life:
> ***bless us and keep us.***

You grew in wisdom and grace,
learning obedience:
> ***bless us and keep us.***

You welcomed little children,
promising them the kingdom of heaven:
> ***bless us and keep us.***

You comforted those who mourned,
grieving for their children:
> ***bless us and keep us.***

You took upon yourself
the suffering of us all:
> ***bless us and keep us.***

Lord Jesus Christ,
you rose from the dead
bringing life eternal:
> ***bless us and keep us.***   ***Amen.***

Gracious God,
speak to us now
the message of your eternal love.
Lift us above our sorrow
to the light and peace
of your presence;
through Jesus Christ our Lord.   ***Amen.***

5   SCRIPTURE READINGS

Hear the Word of God,
written for our help and comfort.

OLD TESTAMENT

As a mother comforts her son
so shall I myself comfort you;
in Jerusalem you will find comfort.

Isaiah 66: 13

Psalms

As a father has compassion on his children,
so the Lord has compassion
on those who fear him;
for he knows how we were made,
he remembers that we are but dust.
The days of a mortal are as grass;
he blossoms like a wild flower in the meadow:
a wind passes over him, and he is gone,
and his place knows him no more.
But the Lord's love is for ever
on those who fear him,
and his righteousness on their posterity,
on those who hold fast to his covenant,
who keep his commandments in mind.

Psalm 103: 13 - 17

The Lord is my shepherd; I shall not want.
He maketh me to lie down in green pastures;
he leadeth me beside the still waters.
He restoreth my soul;
he leadeth me in the paths of righteousness
for his name's sake.

Yea, though I walk
through the valley of the shadow of death,
I will fear no evil;
for thou art with me;
thy rod and staff they comfort me.
Thou preparest a table before me
in the presence of mine enemies;
thou anointest my head with oil;
my cup runneth over.
Surely goodness and mercy shall follow me
all the days of my life;
and I will dwell
in the house of the Lord for ever.   *Psalm 23 (AV)*

or

The Lord is my shepherd; I lack for nothing.
He makes me lie down in green pastures,
he leads me to water where I may rest;
he revives my spirit;
for his name's sake he guides me
in the right paths.
Even were I to walk through a valley
of deepest darkness
I should fear no harm, for you are with me;
your shepherd's staff and crook
afford me comfort.

You spread a table for me
in the presence of my enemies;
you have richly anointed my head with oil,
and my cup brims over.
Goodness and love unfailing will follow me
all the days of my life,
and I shall dwell in the house of the Lord
throughout the years to come.   *Psalm 23*

Epistle

I am convinced that there is nothing
in death or life,
in the realm of spirits or superhuman powers,
in the world as it is or the world as it shall be,
in the forces of the universe,
in heights or depths –
nothing in all creation that can separate us
from the love of God in Christ Jesus our Lord.

Romans 8: 38 - 39

Consider how great is the love
which the Father has bestowed on us
in calling us his children!
For that is what we are.
The reason why the world does not recognize us
is that it has not known him.
Dear friends, we are now God's children;
what we shall be has not yet been disclosed,
but we know that when Christ appears
we shall be like him,
because we shall see him as he is.
As he is pure,
everyone who has grasped this hope
makes himself pure.

1 John 3: 1 - 3

I heard a loud voice
proclaiming from the throne:
'Now at last
God has his dwelling with mankind!
He will dwell among them
and they shall be his people,
and God himself will be with them.
He will wipe every tear from their eyes;
there shall be an end to death,

and to mourning and crying and pain;
for the old order has passed away!'

Revelation 21: 3 - 4

Gospel

The disciples came to Jesus and asked,
'Who is the greatest in the kingdom of heaven?'
He called a child,
set him in front of them, and said,
'Truly I tell you:
unless you turn round and become like children,
you will never enter the kingdom of heaven.
Whoever humbles himself
and becomes like this child
will be the greatest in the kingdom of heaven,
and whoever receives one such child
in my name receives me.
See that you do not despise
one of these little ones;
I tell you, they have their angels in heaven,
who look continually
on the face of my heavenly Father.

What do you think?
Suppose someone has a hundred sheep,
and one of them strays,
does he not leave the ninety-nine on the hillside
and go in search of the one that strayed?
Truly I tell you: if he should find it,
he is more delighted over that sheep
than over the ninety-nine that did not stray.
In the same way,
it is not your heavenly Father's will
that one of these little ones should be lost.

St Matthew 18: 1 - 5, 10 - 14

They brought children for Jesus to touch.
The disciples rebuked them,
but when Jesus saw it he was indignant,
and said to them,
'Let the children come to me;
for the kingdom of God belongs to such as these.
Truly I tell you:
whoever does not accept the kingdom of God
like a child will never enter it.'
And he put his arms round them,
laid his hands on them,
and blessed them.

St Mark 10: 13 - 16

6   ADDRESS

7   PRAYER

Let us pray.

God of all grace and comfort,
we thank you for *N* . . . ,
and for the place *he* gained
in all our hearts.
We thank you
for the love in which *he* was conceived
and for the care with which *he* was surrounded.
As we remember times of tears and laughter,
we thank you for the love we shared
because of *him*.
We commend *him* to your safe keeping.
Rest eternal grant unto *him*.
Let light perpetual shine upon *him*.

Eternal God,
in Jesus Christ you promise eternal life

to us and to our children.
We thank you for the assurance and hope
that *N . . .'s* life is complete in you
and that *he* is living with you now
in the love and joy of your family in heaven.
Help us to know that together
we are enfolded in your love for ever.

God of unchanging love,
you are able
to bring good out of evil
and to raise up life from the dead.
May we know your saving peace
in the days to come,
and find new life in your eternal love.

We pray for those
to whom great sorrow and loss has come,
for *X . . .* and *Y . . .* (*parents*),
and *Z . . .* (*sister, brother*),
for the grandparents and all the family.
By the precious memories they share,
draw them closer to one another;
by the assurance that *N . . .*
is safe in your keeping,
draw them closer to you.
May they find the healing power of Christ
in all their grief and pain.

Bless us all,
friends, neighbours, (school friends and teachers),
that, by bearing one another's burdens,
we may show the love of Christ.
Gather us, with all your children,
into your everlasting arms,
so that, even when we cannot understand,

we may be filled with the light and comfort
of your presence.

God our Father,
you know our thoughts and share our sorrows.
Lead us out of desolation
to the caring comfort of your love.
When we forget what happiness is,
renew in us fresh springs of hope.
When we feel bereft of peace,
restore our hearts and calm our fears.
And when we come at last to our departing,
bring us home with you forever,
the family of God complete;
through Jesus Christ our Lord.

Amen.

Our Father . . .

8 BLESSING *if the Committal is elsewhere*

9 COMMITTAL

At the place of committal, all stand.

The minister says:

Jesus said,
It is not your heavenly Father's will
that one of these little ones should be lost.
I am the resurrection and the life.
Whoever has faith in me shall live,
even though he dies;
and no one who lives and has faith in me
shall ever die.

at the grave

N . . . is in the care of almighty God.
We now commit *his* body to the ground,
earth to earth, ashes to ashes, dust to dust,
in sure and certain hope of eternal life;
through Jesus Christ, who died, was buried,
and rose again for us,
and is alive and reigns for evermore.

Amen.

in the crematorium

N . . . is in the care of almighty God.
We now commit *his* body to the elements,
ashes to ashes, dust to dust,
in sure and certain hope of eternal life;
through Jesus Christ, who died, was buried,
and rose again for us,
and is alive and reigns for evermore. **Amen.**

The Lamb who is at the centre of the throne
will be their shepherd
and will guide them
to springs of the water of life;
and God will wipe every tear from their eyes.

Revelation 7: 17

God will show us the path of life:
in his presence there is fullness of joy,
and at his right hand
there are pleasures for evermore. *Psalm 16: 11*

10 PRAYER

Let us pray.

Loving God,
your Son our Saviour
put his arms around the children
and blessed them.
We thank you that you have received *N* . . .
into your never-failing care,
and welcomed him into the light and love
of your presence.

or

Heavenly Father,
we bless you for the assurance that *N* . . .
is safe in your keeping
and that you have welcomed *him*
into the light and love of your presence.

Comfort all who have loved *him* here on earth,
with the knowledge that you have called *him*
to yourself
and will keep *him* safe now and for ever;
and bring us at the last
to your everlasting kingdom;
through Jesus Christ our Lord.

Living God,
though our thoughts may linger here,
we believe that *N* . . .
has made a new beginning,
with your mercy and love still around *him*.
Strengthened by this assurance,
help us to return to the tasks that await us,
resolved to be faithful to you
and true to one another;
for the sake of Jesus Christ our Lord.

Amen.

Almighty God,
we commend ourselves and all dear to us,
wherever they may be,
to your gracious protection.
Guard us in life and in death,
that whether we wake or sleep,
we may live together with you;
through Jesus Christ our Lord.

Amen.

11 HYMN

12 BLESSING

The peace of God,
which is beyond all understanding,
guard your hearts and your thoughts
in Christ Jesus.

And the blessing of God almighty,
the Father, the Son, and the Holy Spirit,
be with you.

Amen.

Order for the Funeral of a Still-born Child

1 INTRODUCTION

These, or similar words, may be used.

We gather here
on what is for all of us a sad occasion.
We were looking forward
to a time of joy and happiness,
and now there are tears and grief.
We are left with a feeling of emptiness.
All that has happened seems futile and pointless.
Our minds are filled with questions
to which there appear to be no answers:
so many things we do not know;
so many things we do not understand.

But there are some truths we do know.
We know that the God who made us, loves us;
that he loves us always;
that, through his Son Jesus Christ,
he has promised never to leave us
nor forsake us.
And we know also,
as others before us have found,
that his strength is available for us,
especially at those times when we feel
that we have no strength of our own.
These promises are found in God's Word.

2   SCRIPTURE READINGS

Some of these Lessons may be read:

> Like a shepherd he will tend his flock
> and with his arm keep them together;
> he will carry the lambs in his bosom.
>
> *Isaiah 40: 11*

> The Lord is my shepherd,
> I lack for nothing.
> He makes me lie down in green pastures,
> he leads me to water where I may rest;
> he revives my spirit;
> for his name's sake he guides me
> in the right paths.
> Even were I to walk
> through a valley of deepest darkness
> I should fear no harm,
> for you are with me;
> your shepherd's staff and crook
> afford me comfort.
>
> You spread a table for me
> in the presence of my enemies;
> you have richly anointed my head with oil,
> and my cup brims over.
>
> Goodness and love unfailing
> will follow me all the days of my life,
> and I shall dwell in the house of the Lord
> throughout the years to come.
>
> *Psalm 23*

> Love is patient and kind.
> Love envies no one,

is never boastful,
never conceited, never rude;
love is never selfish, never quick to take offence.
Love keeps no score of wrongs,
takes no pleasure in the sins of others,
but delights in the truth.
There is nothing love cannot face;
there is no limit to its faith,
its hope, its endurance.
Love will never come to an end.
At present we see only puzzling reflections
in a mirror,
but one day we shall see face to face.
My knowledge now is partial;
then it will be whole,
like God's knowledge of me.
There are three things that last for ever:
faith, hope and love;
and the greatest of the three is love.

1 Corinthians 13: 4 - 8, 12 - 13

God has said,
'I will never leave you or desert you.'
So we can take courage and say,
'The Lord is my helper, I will not fear;
what can man do to me?'

Hebrews 13: 5, 6

Jesus says,
It is not your heavenly Father's will
that one of these little ones should be lost.

St Matthew 18: 14

Jesus says,
Let the children come to me;
for the kingdom of God belongs to such as these.

Truly I tell you:
whoever does not accept the kingdom of God
like a child will never enter it.
And he put his arms round them,
laid his hands on them, and blessed them.

St Mark 10: 13 - 16

These reassuring words
have brought comfort and strength
to the friends of God through the ages.
May we also know the truth of his promises,
and find in him the strength and peace we need.

3 PRAYERS

Let us pray.

Some of these prayers may be said,
ending with the prayer at e.:

a. Gracious God,
we thank you for the love
in which *N* . . . was conceived,
and for the love of the home
into which *he* was to be born.

We pray that the love
which *his* parents have for each other
may grow and deepen
as a result of this experience.

Give us grace, in patience and understanding,
to listen to each other,
and to help one another
in the days to come.

b. Lord Jesus Christ,
   you took little children into your arms
   and laid your hands upon them
   and blessed them.

   Assure us that you have taken our child *N* . . .
   into your arms and into your care,
   and that *he* and we together
   are enfolded in your love.

c. Almighty God, creator and keeper of life,
   we acknowledge that our child *N* . . .
   is your child,
   loved since before the foundation of the world.

   Grant us such trust
   in the finished work of your Son our Saviour
   that we shall look with hope
   towards a full knowledge of *N* . . . ,
   whose earthly life we have so little shared
   but who is now complete with Christ in you.

   We commend *him* to your safe keeping.
   Rest eternal grant unto *him*.
   Let light perpetual shine upon *him*.

d. Heavenly Father,
   you alone can heal our broken hearts;
   you alone can wipe away the tears
   that well up inside us;
   you alone can give us the peace we need;
   you alone can strengthen us to carry on.

   We ask you to be near those
   whose time of joy has been turned into sadness.

ORDER FOR THE FUNERAL OF A STILL-BORN CHILD

Assure them that with you
nothing is wasted or incomplete,
and uphold them with your tender love.

Supported by your strength,
may our love for one another
be deepened by the knowledge
of your love for us all.

e. Loving God,
amid all our questions,
help us to trust you.
In our time of darkness,
shine into our lives
with the light of your presence.

Our Father . . .

4   COMMITTAL

at the grave
We have entrusted (this little child) *N* . . .
into the hands of God.
We now commit *his* body to the ground,
earth to earth, ashes to ashes, dust to dust,
in sure and certain hope
of the resurrection to eternal life;
through Jesus Christ, who died, was buried,
and rose again for us,
and is alive and reigns for evermore.   **Amen.**

in the crematorium
We have entrusted (this little child) *N* . . .
into the hands of God.
We now commit *his* body to be cremated,
ashes to ashes, dust to dust,

in sure and certain hope
of the resurrection to eternal life;
through Jesus Christ, who died, was buried,
and rose again for us,
and is alive and reigns for evermore.

Amen.

5   BLESSING

The peace of God,
which is beyond all understanding,
guard your hearts and your thoughts
in Christ Jesus.

And the blessing of God almighty,
the Father, the Son, and the Holy Spirit,
be with you.

Amen.

Order for the Interment or Scattering of Ashes

1 SCRIPTURE SENTENCES

The eternal God is our refuge,
and underneath are the everlasting arms.

Deuteronomy 33: 27 (AV)

Trust in the Lord at all times;
pour out your hearts before him;
God is our shelter.

Psalm 62: 8

God so loved the world
that he gave his only Son,
that everyone who has faith in him
may not perish but have eternal life.

St John 3: 16

There is nothing in death or life,
in the world as it is or the world as it shall be,
nothing in all creation that can separate us
from the love of God in Christ Jesus our Lord.

Romans 8: 38, 39

Praised be the God and Father
of our Lord Jesus Christ!
In his great mercy
by the resurrection of Jesus Christ from the dead,
he gave us new birth into a living hope,

the hope of an inheritance,
reserved in heaven for you,
which nothing can destroy or spoil or wither.

1 Peter 1: 3 - 4

The souls of the righteous are in God's hand;
no torment will touch them.
They are at peace. *Wisdom 3: 1, 3*

2 PRAYERS

God, the Lord of life and conqueror of death,
you are our help in every time of trouble.
We thank you for the assurance of the Gospel,
that in your keeping
the souls of the faithful
find lasting peace and joy,
and that though we see our loved ones no more
they are safe with you.

Comfort all who mourn.
May our memories of *N . . .*
be a consolation for the present
and a strength for the future.
By the glorious resurrection of your Son,
confirm in us the hope of eternal life,
and enable us to put our whole trust
in your goodness and mercy;
through the same Jesus Christ our Lord.

Amen.

3 SCRIPTURE READINGS

If it is for this life only
that Christ has given us hope,
we of all people are most to be pitied.

But the truth is,
Christ was raised to life –
the firstfruits of the harvest of the dead.
For since it was a man
who brought death into the world,
a man also brought resurrection of the dead.
As in Adam all die,
so in Christ all will be brought to life;
but each in proper order:
Christ the firstfruits,
and afterwards, at his coming,
those who belong to Christ.
Then comes the end,
when he delivers up the kingdom
to God the Father,
after deposing every sovereignty,
authority, and power.
For he is destined to reign
until God has put all enemies under his feet;
and the last enemy to be deposed is death.

1 Corinthians 15: 19 - 26

There are heavenly bodies and earthly bodies;
and the splendour of the heavenly bodies
is one thing,
the splendour of the earthly, another.
The sun has a splendour of its own,
the moon another splendour,
and the stars yet another;
and one star differs from another in brightness.
So it is with the resurrection of the dead:
what is sown as a perishable thing
is raised imperishable.
Sown in humiliation, it is raised in glory;
sown in weakness, it is raised in power;
sown a physical body,

it is raised a spiritual body.

1 Corinthians 15: 40 - 44

No wonder we do not lose heart!
Though our outward humanity is in decay,
yet day by day
we are inwardly renewed.
Our troubles are slight and short-lived,
and their outcome is an eternal glory
which far outweighs them,
provided our eyes are fixed,
not on the things that are seen,
but on the things that are unseen;
for what is seen is transient,
what is unseen is eternal.
We know that if the earthly frame
that houses us today is demolished,
we possess a building which God has provided –
a house not made by human hands,
eternal and in heaven.

2 Corinthians 4: 16 - 5: 1

4 INTERMENT *or* SCATTERING

The Lord says,
'Do not be afraid.
I am the first and the last,
and I am the living One;
I was dead
and now I am alive for evermore.'

Revelation 1: 18

We have entrusted *N* . . .
to God's eternal keeping.
We now commit *his* ashes to the ground
(*to the elements*),

in sure and certain hope
of the resurrection to eternal life
through Jesus Christ our Lord,
who died, was buried, and rose again for us,
and is alive and reigns for ever and ever.

Amen.

5 PRAYERS

Let us pray.

Eternal God,
by your dear Son's rising from the dead
you have destroyed the power of death.
In you the dead find life for ever,
and the faithful
who served you on earth
praise you for all eternity in heaven.

As we return to our tasks,
cheer us by the hope of everlasting life
and support us by the sure love
of your guiding hand.
Bring us at the last,
with all the faithful,
to the full knowledge of your love
and the unclouded vision of your glory;
through Jesus Christ our Lord.   *Amen.*

6 BLESSING

The peace of God,
which is beyond all understanding,
guard your hearts and your thoughts
in Christ Jesus.

And the blessing of God almighty,
Father, Son, and Holy Spirit,
be with you.

Amen.